What Our Readers Have Said...

Applicability

"These books are great tools that should be used as guidelines for our everyday supervisory practices. You need to take the time to do a short self-evaluation when reading them."

•

"The things and problems we deal with everyday are discussed in these books."

•

Convenience

"I like this because I can take them with me to read at a convenient time. I feel the little time I have to spend in the office is best use on activities that directly relate to revenue opportunities. I like the short amount of time it takes to keep up with these."

•

"I just read each book, and then file it for future reference."

•

"I like the fact that the format allows the books to be reviewed as time permits. All work has been conducted on personal, evening/weekend time."

•

Challenge

"My thought is that the real value of these books comes into effect when doing the action plans."

•

"The challenge when I think a specific topic does not apply is to find a way to make it apply."

•

Clarity

"Short and sweet. These books are easy to comprehend."

•

"These books are very easy to read and clearly outlined."

•

"Easy to use, understand, and reference if needed."

•

Relevance

"I have enjoyed reading these books. They are relevant to today's work environment and the ongoing change in the way we manage our workforce."

•

"I believe the contents of the Pinpoint series are excellent. It causes one to reflect on the daily dynamics in working with oneself as well as with management and peers."

•

"I do feel that these books have been very helpful to me at my job."

•

"I do enjoy reading each of theses books and it gives some real thought to its instruction."

•

Handling Angry & Hostile Customers

Pinpoint Customer Service Skill Development Training Series

TIMOTHY F. BEDNARZ

BUSINESS PRESS

Pinpoint Customer Service Skill Development Training Series
"Handling Angry & Hostile Customers"
Timothy F. Bednarz

Graphic design: Monika Pawlak

Majorium Business Press
2025 Main Street
Stevens Point, WI 54481
715.342.1018 • 800.654.4935

Copyright © 2011 Timothy F. Bednarz, Ph.D. All rights reserved. No part of this publication may be reproduced, distributed or transmitted in any form or by any means, including photocopying, recording, or other electronic or mechanical methods, without author's written permission.

ISBN 978-1-882181-26-1

Printed in the United States of America

Introduction

The Pinpoint Customer Service Skill Development Training Series is designed for targeted training and education regarding increased improvement in a specific skill or competency.

Each book within this series is designed to be easy to use, understand and apply to your job. It can be used as a basis for training individuals, as a discussion guide or as a personal training tool.

Each chapter within this book discusses a specific concept. When you have completed all eight chapters you should have a 360º perspective of the topic.

Additionally, each chapter is divided into specific sections:

- The first section provides you with an overview of the topic
- The Implications section discusses why the concept is important, and why it is important to learn and apply.
- The Strategies, Tips & Techniques to Apply section teaches how to use and apply the particular concept to your work.
- The Points to Ponder section gives you something to think about or to be discussed with a group setting. These are questions not meant to be immediately answered, but to be pondered over time.
- The Training Activity section provides you with the tools to transfer what you have learned to your job. It is designed to help create an action plan to effectively apply the concept.

Each of the topics in this series is time-tested and proven in the marketplace. They have been used by thousands of employees as training tools. Many of the users have commented that what made these books valuable, was the ability to refer to them when a problem surfaced. They indicated that they remembered reading about the exact problem. They referred back to these books and found an appropriate solution.

You will find them equally valuable as a resource in your professional development library.

Table of Contents

1. What Angry and Hostile Customers Want and Need 1

2. The Nature of Angry, Hostile and Abusive Behavior 5

3. Triggering Events 11

4. Major Rules of Hostile Interaction 15

5. Diffusing the Angry and Hostile Customer 19

6. Maintaining Self-Control 23

7. Cooperative Language 27

8. Verbal Self-Defensive Techniques 31

LEARNING OBJECTIVES:

- To identify reasons why customers are more demanding and increasingly hostile.
- To understand the causes of customer anger and hostility.
- How to handle angry and hostile customers.
- To understand how to handle the stress associated with angry and hostile customers.

1

What Angry and Hostile Customers Want and Need

Anger is an emotion that belongs to another person and is hard to affect directly. Hostile and abusive behavior is an altogether different story. Service representatives can and must focus their efforts on reducing the amount of verbal and nonverbal hostility they experience.

In all service environments, customers want their problems solved, and have initiated contact with a particular goal in mind. Unfortunately, in certain situations, the demands they place on the service representative can be unreasonable, highly specific and involve immediate action. As they have to work within the constraints of their job, service representatives cannot always meet these demands. Often they don't have the authority or even the ability to meet the needs or wants of customers. In these and other situations, the service representative can become the target of a customer's anger and rage against the company.

IMPLICATIONS — WHAT THIS MEANS TO YOU

It is important for service representatives to understand that individuals choose their own emotional states. Their feelings of anger belong to them and are not the service representative's responsibility. However, it *is* the service representative's responsibility to ensure that they don't knowingly or unknowingly do something to provoke the customer's anger and hostility.

Service representatives accept the fact that people have the right to be angry at times. However, they do not have the right to take their anger out on the service representative, especially when they have done nothing to contribute to it.

STRATEGIES, TIPS & TECHNIQUES TO APPLY

When service representatives deal with angry customers, they will likely have asked themselves, "What does this person want from me?" In certain situations, they may have even asked the customer this question. This basic but important question invariably has a number of answers, the knowledge of which will help service representatives calm an angry person and reduce the hostility directed at them. Service representatives can address a number of psychological needs to ease hostile behavior:

Help

Despite their personal attitude and demeanor, hostile and angry individuals want service representatives to be helpful—even if they can't solve their entire problem. If they see service representatives making a genuine effort on their behalf, they are much less likely to be hostile towards them personally. In most cases they appreciate the effort being made and are much less likely to harass the service representative.

Anger and hostility mask an individual's helplessness with their situation. If they feel that a service representative is not being helpful, or doesn't seem to care about their problems and concerns, this infuriates them and fuels their hostility.

Choices

Many hostile customers feel they have no options and are trapped in the system. Even if they are the cause of their own problems, they feel cornered and lash out at the service representative.

One way to defuse a hostile situation is to provide choices whenever possible. In most service situations there are always choices that can be offered. Research shows that customers respond much more favorably when offered alternatives. It reduces their sense of helplessness and allays a highly charged, emotional situation.

Acknowledgement

One of the most important things an angry customer wants is to be acknowledged. A common pitfall many service representatives encounter when dealing with an angry customer is to ignore the feelings being expressed and to shift immediately into a problem solving (or much worse, defensive) mode. While many service representatives might consider immediate problem solving to be efficient, customers perceive this approach as uncaring, unfeeling and unhelpful. This results in increased anger and hostility.

It is important for service representatives to understand that angry individuals want the service representative to make an effort to understand the situation and their emotional reactions to it – to "walk a mile in their shoes." When service representatives acknowledge that a person is upset and a problem has occurred – provided that the acknowledgement is phrased and toned correctly – this will often calm them down.

Escalation

When a customer has experienced less than optimal treatment that causes them to become angry, logic dictates that failure to address their source of frustration will only increase their hostility and abusive behavior. If service representatives fail to recognize what is occurring and do not interrupt it immediately, the situation will become a crisis.

Within the service environment, escalation into a hostile situation does not have to occur. It is important for service representatives to be aware of their behavior in contributing to this cycle.

Hostile situations don't always start with abusive and hostile behavior. Even a relatively benign situation can escalate very quickly if a person antagonizes the other with his or her responses. When one or more people are angry in the first place, there is a far greater chance of escalation.

In many instances, escalation can be stopped provided service representatives are able to step back from the situation, handle it professionally, and not get baited into arguments or other negative behaviors that will only serve to fuel hostility.

> ### POINTS TO PONDER — SOMETHING TO THINK ABOUT
>
> 1. In your experience, what typically triggers and escalates hostility in a customer?
> 2. What do you do to defuse a situation that is escalating quickly into a hostile and angry one?

TRAINING ACTIVITY — APPLICATION & ACTION PLAN

Service representatives who recognize the customer's wants and provide for them can significantly reduce their hostility.

1. Identify ways to demonstrate helpfulness to your customer, especially that go above and beyond what is expected of you as a service representative.
2. Identify ways to provide customers with options and choices they might not be aware of and that may diffuse any emotional responses toward your company.
3. Identify ways to acknowledge a customer's feelings, emotions and problems when interacting with them.
4. Review the first three steps and determine how you can expand your service in each of these areas to become more helpful and service-oriented.

2

The Nature of Angry, Hostile and Abusive Behavior

The concept of hostile and abusive behavior almost always has to do with controlling the situation. When service representatives understand the basis of these behaviors, they become aware of the actions needed to defuse the customer's anger and take charge of the situation.

The purpose of hostile and abusive behavior is to control or manipulate the environment. In most service situations, this means it is intended to control the service representative, influence their reactions and manipulate them into doing whatever the customer demands. Often these irrational behaviors have been learned and ingrained in childhood.

■ IMPLICATIONS — WHAT THIS MEANS TO YOU

Service representatives will notice similarities in the tactics and attacks people use in hostile situations, including a common body language, vocabulary and tone. Because of this, service representatives can understand that abusive behavior has its own rules. This will help them understand what to do when attacked and how to defuse the situation.

STRATEGIES, TIPS & TECHNIQUES TO APPLY

Angry behavior is not always the same as hostile and abusive behavior, and it is important for service representatives to distinguish between the two in order to deal effectively with their customers.

Anger

Anger is an internal state experienced by customers. An angry individual experiences physiological changes, some of which are visible, but in most cases, invisible. Service representatives should understand that people choose their own emotional states. Feelings of anger—or for that matter any other feelings—belong to them and not to the service representative.

People express their anger in a variety of ways. Some raise their voices and become animated, while others silently turn red and appear frustrated. Mild expressions of anger should be acceptable and are simply a way for an individual to vent their emotional frustration. If service representatives are to be effective, they need to be reasonable and allow angry customers some latitude in their behavior before they deem it unacceptable. Service representatives who are easily offended will find that their personal reaction will often trigger a hostile and abusive situation.

Hostile and Abusive Behavior

Hostile and abusive behavior causes the greatest amount of stress for service representatives. This is because customers utilizing these behaviors tend to use intimidating tactics, including ranting, insulting, and refusing to go away. This is different than angry behavior, which is often acceptable. However, hostile and abusive behavior:
- Keeps the service representative off-balance
- Attempts to manipulate and control the service representative
- Is demeaning and intimidating
- Causes the service representative to feel guilty

What sets hostile and abusive behavior apart from angry behavior is that it is consciously or unconsciously intended to have some or all of the preceding effects. It is important for service representatives to attempt to stop these behaviors as professionally as possible. This includes reducing the anger and defusing the situation as quickly as possible. When this is impossible, it is important that service representatives recognize that the anger belongs to the customer and not to them.

Verbal Abuse

Verbal abuse is an extension of hostile and abusive behaviors and is intended to demean and control the service representative. Verbal abuse can take a great number of forms, from very subtle to obvious. They typically take the form of:
- Persistent swearing and/or yelling
- Explicit or implied sexist or racist comments
- Irrelevant personal remarks
- Personal threats
- Accusations
- Derogatory comments regarding the service representative's competency, knowledge and dedication

Nonverbal Abuse

Nonverbal abuse is communicated through posture, facial expressions, gestures, and other body language. These behaviors may be a relatively normal way of expressing anger. However, they are classified as abusive because they do tend to have a manipulating effect on service representatives and, in many cases, are intended to intimidate or demean them. These behaviors can include:
- Standing in personal space
- Intimidating silence and staring including long eye contact
- Table pounding
- Throwing objects
- Leaning close to or over the service representative
- Angry facial expressions
- Loud sighing
- Pointing and other offensive gestures

Violence

Violence is any activity that is intended to cause, or can cause, physical harm to another individual. Actions include physical contact, such as arm or shoulder grabbing, which can be legally interpreted as assault. Additional actions, such as throwing objects, would be considered violent behavior if there was intent to cause harm or actual harm was done.

However, "acting out" behavior is not considered violent, but abusive and hostile. This would include things like ripping up papers and throwing them or sweeping items off of a desk.

Service representatives should understand that violent behavior rarely occurs for no reason. It is part of a sequence of events that involve verbal abuse. This is why it is important for service representatives to learn how to defuse hostility and verbal abuse before it escalates into the potential for physical violence.

POINTS TO PONDER — SOMETHING TO THINK ABOUT

1. Do you feel that the customer is always right and that it is your responsibility to keep them happy?
2. Do you understand how your personal behavior and reactions to a customer situation can trigger anger and hostility?

TRAINING ACTIVITY — APPLICATION & ACTION PLAN

On a sheet of paper, make a random list of any angry and hostile customer situations that you experienced in the past 30 days.
1. Next to each episode, define it by assigning applicable characteristics:
   - Anger
   - Hostile, abusive behavior

- Verbal abuse
- Nonverbal abuse
- Violence

2. If one or more characteristics were assigned to an event, define the triggering point that escalated the situation.
3. Determine if and how these triggering points could have been avoided.
4. Analyze all of the events and determine how strong a role your behavior had in escalating the angry and hostile situation.

3

Triggering Events

Often the customer is not solely responsible for their abusive behaviors. Service representatives must understand that in a potentially abusive and hostile situation, their personal behaviors have the potential of triggering adverse customer reactions.

Personal attitudes and terse comments can lead to an angry customer getting angrier. It can be difficult to put the best foot forward in every instance when dealing with a customer who is under an enormous amount of stress—or worse, bitter and unhappy in general. Regardless, it is the service representative's job to demonstrate empathy and helpfulness to the customer wherever and whenever humanly possible, and to *always* maintain professionalism. In other words, when a customer contact has deteriorated into chaos, in no way should the representative's behavior be a contributing factor.

▇ IMPLICATIONS – WHAT THIS MEANS TO YOU

Service representatives have the ability to defuse and control a difficult situation in such a way as to allow customers to vent their emotions and then lead them to an accommodating solution. Customers resort to angry and hostile behavior when they feel powerless and out of control. They feel unimportant and that nobody in the company is interested in their problem. While their problem may appear minor to the service representative, it is major to the customer—and they want this acknowledged. When this fails to occur, the service representative's behavior and potentially uncaring attitude can trigger escalating levels of irritation, hostility and abusive behavior. This creates additional stress and problems for both the customer and the company.

▰ STRATEGIES, TIPS & TECHNIQUES TO APPLY

Service representatives must understand how angry and hostile behaviors occur and their part in the escalation of the cycle into a customer crisis.

Initial Contact

When an anxious customer makes their initial contact with a service representative, they are already frustrated and perhaps angry about a product failure or some other event that may have affected their business. The failure can impact their business financially by reducing productivity and effectiveness. The situation may make them feel powerless and fearful of the consequences. This places them in a reactive mode where they are sensitive to the words and actions of the service representative.

In an effort to increase their customer service efficiency, many companies instead place a great number of obstacles in the customer's way of obtaining personal service. Customers may be forced to go through a loop of multiple phone options only to be put on hold when they finally get a live representative. Worse, they may have to leave a voice mail message before they can obtain service. This is irritating. It makes customers feel unimportant and depersonalizes the service experience. They want a solution to their problem, and instead are forced to jump through hoops. The result is an increasingly frustrated and agitated customer who feels they must assert control in order to get an answer.

Employee Response

In many situations where an already frustrated client is supposed to receive service, they instead receive an automatic, apathetic response to their problems. The service representative can appear passive and out of touch – or worse, defensive. This is typified by a wholly unhelpful lack of listening skills, impatience and abrupt answers. In many cases, service representatives feel that they simply do not need to hear it or deal with hostile and angry customers. This immediately places them in a defensive mode, which serves to heighten the customer's irritation.

Customer Reaction

When frustrated and agitated customers are greeted with a fairly cold and bureaucratic response and made to feel unvalued and unimportant, this only exacerbates their frustration. It increases their sense of helplessness and fear that the problem will not be resolved. If the problem is perceived to be fairly serious to the customer and the service representative appears to be uncaring, this increases their aggression and hostility. The situation appears to be spiraling out of the customer's control, and they use this behavior in an attempt to gain control over the situation and the service representative. When service representatives appear unmoved and unresponsive, customers tend to become more aggressive and ultimately abusive.

Employee Reaction

As the situation deteriorates in a downward cycle toward further hostility and anger, the service representative increasingly feels he or she must defend their "turf" or even counterattack the customer. Not surprisingly, this tends to elicit more hostile and angry behavior on the part of the customer. At this point both service representative and customer tend to lose self-control and become highly emotional in their responses. Both become more vocal and aggressive. The service representative, rather than trying to take control of the situation to defuse the customer's agitation and resolve the problem, is seen as part of the problem.

Total Escalation

Once the situation becomes completely out of control, both customers and service representatives trigger additional emotional responses. Irritation leads to angry behavior that escalates to hostility and abusiveness, including verbal abuse and the potential for violence.

In most situations, service representatives are trained to remove themselves from a potentially volatile situation. Once events tend to escalate out of control, most will defer the customer to a supervisor, manager or another service representative trained to handle explosive and potentially violent situations.

POINTS TO PONDER — SOMETHING TO THINK ABOUT

1. Have you experienced situations where a customer contact escalated into a crisis?
2. When faced with an angry and hostile customer, do you automatically become defensive, or are you able to defuse the situation?

TRAINING ACTIVITY — APPLICATION & ACTION PLAN

On a sheet of paper, create a flow chart of the typical service behaviors you employ on a service call.

1. Note a plus or minus sign next to each activity within the flow chart to indicate your personal attitude when dealing with the customer.
2. Identify and circle potential triggering points and events that might elicit a negative response from the customer.
3. Determine how to eliminate these triggering points from your typical service response.
4. Identify positive behaviors to replace these triggering events.
5. Practice these behaviors for a minimum of 30 days to create a positive service habit.

4

Major Rules of Hostile Interaction

Service representatives who deal with irate and angry customers on a frequent basis notice similarities in attacks and tactics. They find that, as there is a finite number of ways people can be hostile, patterns tend to repeat themselves. These methods are learned very early on and are reinforced through adulthood.

■ IMPLICATIONS — WHAT THIS MEANS TO YOU

One of the service representative's primary goals in a difficult situation is to avoid being controlled and manipulated. They must avoid responding to nasty attacks in the manner angry and hostile customers anticipate. If service representatives refuse to be controlled and react in the way that the customer wishes, they can be effective in stopping the personal attacks and in dealing with the customer's emotions.

Hostile behavior appears to follow rules and certain patterns that repeat themselves. If service representatives are aware of this, it will help equip them with what to do when attacked. Otherwise they will find themselves repeatedly manipulated and out of control of the situation.

■ STRATEGIES, TIPS & TECHNIQUES TO APPLY

The major goal of a hostile customer's behavior is to control the service representative and take charge of the entire situation. These individuals want to take the initiative, forcing the service representative to react and respond to them. As long as the belligerent customer can control the conversation, the hostile interaction will likely continue. This diminishes a service representative's effectiveness because they are unable to assist the customer or end the interaction positively.

Baiting is a primary technique hostile customers employ in their bid to maintain control. This consists of behaviors, both verbal and nonverbal, designed to get the service representative to react emotionally. Once they do, the service representative has lost the initiative to the hostile customer. Baiting is used to upset service representatives and keep them off-balance by angering and/or intimidating them. Baiting comments are typically blaming, demeaning and threatening. Service representatives are made to feel helpless and unable to control the situation.

When service representatives "take the bait," hostile customers know they have found gaps in their armor. They now know how to maintain control using additional manipulative behaviors. If customers know they are able to upset service representatives, their behavior and attacks will continue. The key point service representatives must understand is that hostile and angry customers *expect* them to take the bait. This is an essential rule of the hostility game.

As the hostile customer and service representative respond to one another, the situation begins to spin out of control. As the conversation gets more destructive and potentially abusive, focus on the original problem is lost.

Service representatives must learn to operate within a different set of rules. The first is not to play the hostile customer's games on his or her terms. Baiting is a game that is defined by the attacker. Service representatives must recognize baiting as just that – a game intended to control and irritate them.

Service representatives should further understand that when people are baited and attacked, they typically respond with one of two automatic responses:

Defensiveness

Most individuals who are personally attacked will have a natural tendency to defend themselves. However, there is a pronounced difference between defense and defensiveness. Defense implies a professional assertiveness in which an individual respectfully, yet firmly stands their ground. Defensiveness is, on the other hand, a posture of helplessness that does nothing whatever to advance a sale or solve a problem. It shifts the focus to the service representative, which is precisely where it should not be, least of all when dealing with an attacking customer.

Serving only to embolden attacks, defensiveness often takes the form of statements such as:
- I'm doing the best I can.
- I know what I'm doing!
- I'm sorry– we're short-staffed.

Service representatives should again note that defensive statements almost always contain the word "I" or "we." These are intended to deflect personal and emotional attacks away from them, but in fact achieve the opposite effect. Even friendly customers obviously and understandably care very little whether the sales rep is short-staffed. The bottom line rests in the fact that defensiveness, especially with hostile customers, will never achieve the desired result, and instead will very likely worsen the situation.

Counterattack

This rule of engagement specifies that when service representatives are personally attacked, they will retaliate by making comments or remarks about the customer such as:
- You have no right to talk to me like that.
- You don't know what you're talking about.
- If your behavior continues, I will hang up.

The service representative should note that counterattacking comments almost always contain the word "you." While these comments focus on the customer, they are an emotional response. If service representatives make similar unprofessional counterattacks, they are again playing by the hostile customer's rules. This is what hostile customers expect, and they will again become emboldened in their attack. Just as with defensiveness, service representatives who fall into this trap will ultimately lose.

POINTS TO PONDER — SOMETHING TO THINK ABOUT

1. Have you experienced situations in which you have been baited by hostile customers and manipulated into an emotional response?
2. Do you have a tendency to immediately react to angry and hostile situations without forethought, or do you take the time to collect your thoughts and formulate a professional response?

■ TRAINING ACTIVITY — APPLICATION & ACTION PLAN

Over the next several days, observe the behaviors of hostile and angry individuals and customers.
1. Look for ways adults express their hostility and anger.
2. Think of ways children express their hostility and anger.
3. Determine the similarities between the two.
4. Note your own personal behavior when you get angry and determine whether your behavior is adult or unprofessional.

5

Diffusing the Angry and Hostile Customer

When service representatives communicate with hostile accounts, the customer will often "take the floor," refusing to listen. In such a volatile customer contact, the service representative's first goal is to defuse and regain control of the situation. Unless hostile customers are moved to stop ranting, there is no likelihood of a positive outcome being arrived at.

Angry and hostile customers employ specific behaviors to intimidate service representatives and gain control of the situation. These individuals assume an attacking position, refusing to let the service representative talk, peppering him or her with questions, demands and even insults. When service representatives understand this, they can also employ behaviors that allow them to defuse the situation and compel the customer to become more cooperative, less emotional and more rational.

IMPLICATIONS — WHAT THIS MEANS TO YOU

Customer attacks cause service representatives to become defensive, angry and off-balance. Service representatives will find that, without the nuances of nonverbal communication, this phenomenon becomes pronounced when dealing with customers over the phone. Regardless of the circumstance, service representatives need to bring hostile customers to the point where they are willing to stop talking and listen.

■ STRATEGIES, TIPS & TECHNIQUES TO APPLY

Service representatives must behave in ways that send subtle messages to the hostile customer that the use of antagonism will not work. Throughout the situation, service representatives must acknowledge and refocus the customer on the problem and away from their feelings and emotions.

Additionally, service representatives should understand that there are basic principles of behavior involved when attempting to defuse a hostile situation:

Allow Venting

The first step service representatives must take is to allow angry and hostile customers to vent their frustrations. While this does not imply that they are to passively stand by as they are being personally attacked, human beings do however have a natural need to release frustration. When this is directed toward the representative's product or handling of the account—whether with or without basis in fact—it should be allowed, as this will greatly increase the odds of the customer then thinking rationally and an amicable solution being arrived at.

Avoid 'Red Tape'

Service representatives must understand that they often represent an organization steeped in bureaucracy, and that this condition is in part what has made the hostile customer feel helpless to begin with. Therefore, the more bureaucratic that service representatives appear, the more likely it will further frustrate the customer. Rather than being viewed as an empowered individual with readily available solutions, service representatives seem to be a part of yet another lumbering bureaucratic colossus. They are perceived more as part of a machine than individuals with answers. If service representatives can personalize themselves as "solution brokers" unfettered by cumbersome and time-consuming processes, anxious customers are less likely to direct hostile behavior at them.

Gentle vs. Assertive Approach

Service representatives must understand that each individual they deal with is unique; some will respond well to a gentle approach, while others will require a more assertive tack.

In either case, it is important for service representatives not to be aggressive or passive, but assertive with customers. They must conduct themselves in a self-assured manner by talking confidently, calmly and firmly. Too forceful an approach leads to confrontation and arguments. On the other hand, excessive passivity will invite hostile customers to intimidate them. Service representatives must rely on their judgment and experience to strike the proper balance in interacting with each individual customer.

Control Emotions and Avoid Escalation

The worst possible thing service representatives can do with hostile customers is lose control of their emotions. They must always keep their personal reactions in check—especially when being baited by the customer. Failure to do so enables the customer to continue with their hostile behaviors. Service representatives should further understand that while they are allowed to be angry and upset with the customer, they are not allowed to take it out on them.

It is important for service representatives to preempt any angry customer attacks by immediately taking control of the situation. This typically means they are the first person to speak and to empathize before angry customers have a chance to launch their attack. If they relinquish control over the situation, they will be unable to produce a positive outcome. Conversely, the earlier service representatives can defuse a situation, the easier it will be to avoid escalating and triggering events that further complicate the service process.

Focus

It is important for service representatives to maintain their focus on the customer's problems during the entire contact. While it is important they continue to acknowledge what the customer is feeling and experiencing, undue attention should not be focused on emotional responses. They must maintain a balance in demonstrating attentiveness and understanding without going into the depth of the customer's feelings and experiences. They acknowledge them, refocus the customer back on his or her problem, and move on to solutions.

The Customer's Perspective

Service representatives proficient in defusing hostile situations are able to look at their behavior from the customer's perspective. Many service representatives who show little or no regard for how their words and actions are being perceived may feel they are being helpful, when in fact what they are saying or doing does not come across at all as intended. When they "step outside of themselves" to view their behavior from an external perspective, they can see how it appears to the customer and make any needed modifications.

> **POINTS TO PONDER — SOMETHING TO THINK ABOUT**
>
> 1. In what manner do you personalize yourself with your customers so that they treat you as a solution-oriented individual and not an object buried in bureaucracy?
> 2. In what ways do you remain assertive with customers and avoid being overly aggressive or passive?

TRAINING ACTIVITY — APPLICATION & ACTION PLAN

Identify a particularly intense and hostile customer contact you recently experienced.

1. Recall ways you allowed the customer to vent his or her emotions or feelings.
2. Think of the specific steps that you employed to diffuse the situation.
3. Identify any phrases or actions that may have contributed to an escalation of the problem.
4. Determine how successful you were in controlling both the customer and the situation.
5. Analyze the entire experience and determine future actions you will take and/or avoid in similar circumstances.

6

Maintaining Self-Control

Hostile and angry customers often say things that are personally demeaning or insulting. One of the most difficult aspects when dealing with them is maintaining control over personal responses and reactions. When service representatives allow themselves to get angry and convey that anger to the customer, the situation will deteriorate further.

IMPLICATIONS — WHAT THIS MEANS TO YOU

Deterioration of self-restraint does not have to lead to a complete loss of control. In most instances, service representatives don't lose control to the point where they become verbally abusive. However, it is fairly common to lose a degree of restraint. When this occurs, service representatives often use a tone of voice or phrases that are provocative. In some instances they might mirror the customer's behavior and treat him or her in the same abusive manner.

STRATEGIES, TIPS & TECHNIQUES TO APPLY

This is important for service representatives to understand, as the loss of self-control only creates additional hostility. Emotional reactions are triggered, further escalating and intensifying the situation. As the pace of the situation quickens, neither party listens to what is said.

Left unchecked, a more dangerous crisis situation develops.

It is neither appropriate nor healthy for service representatives to exhibit these self-defeating behaviors.

When service representatives understand the motivation and techniques employed by hostile customers to intimidate and gain control of the contact, they are better prepared to deal with it and maintain self-control. The following techniques are proven to help service representatives maintain self-control in the face of hostility:

Identifying Trigger Points

Service representatives must identify the triggering points or hot spots that elicit an emotional response from clients. This is the first step to maintaining and improving their self-control. Everyone has specific trigger points. Varying from individual to individual, people's trigger points are based upon their personal experiences and background.

Examples of personal triggering points include:

Words

- Sexism
- Racism
- Profanity
- Suggestions of incompetence
- Suggestions of an uncaring attitude
- Manipulation of guilt

Tone

- Whining
- Yelling
- Sarcasm
- Patronizing

Actions

- Finger-pointing

- Arm-waving
- Waving finger or hands in face
- Pounding on desk
- Door slamming
- Slowing down responses

Angry customers use intimidation in a bid to gain control of the situation. They use baiting tactics to elicit a knee-jerk reaction. If customers are successful, they get service representatives to respond quickly and without thinking. These hasty responses are often incorrect, inappropriate and unprofessional.

The most appropriate course of action is for service representatives to slow down and delay their reply. This enables a filtering out of gut reaction responses that would otherwise trigger additional emotional reactions. Just as one ought wait at least one day before sending an emotionally charged letter or other written communication, so in discourse smaller-scale delays are required before responding to specific comments.

Service representatives must train themselves in the discipline of not responding immediately when confronted in an angry and hostile situation. This can be learned, but it does take time. It is always helpful to count to two or three and/or take at least one deep breath before responding (while careful to not let the breath escape as a sigh).

Timeouts

When service representatives feel themselves getting upset, or hear themselves using an inpatient tone of voice, they should arrange a quick timeout. In many instances they can take a moment to look for a file, get the customer a cup of coffee or do something to break the routine. When on the phone, this may mean putting the customer on hold for an instant, taking a deep breath, then resuming the conversation.

'Self-Talks'

Service representatives can use positive self-talk techniques to maintain a proper perspective. Some examples include:
- This attack is not directed at me personally, the customer is angry with

the company.
- I'm not going to stoop to that.
- I refuse to react to this baiting.
- I can handle this.
- I refuse to let them see me sweat.

Service representatives who create and use their own self-talk will be better able to stay in control during difficult situations.

POINTS TO PONDER — SOMETHING TO THINK ABOUT

1. What techniques do you employ to maintain self-control in a hostile and angry situation?
2. Do you find yourself using positive or negative self-talk during difficult and hostile situations?

TRAINING ACTIVITY — APPLICATION & ACTION PLAN

1. Identify the triggering words, tones and actions that tend to elicit a hasty response on your part.
2. Think of ways to incorporate a delay in order to allow your emotions to cool in both phone and face-to-face dealings with your customers.
3. Be sure to use these techniques in your contacts in order to maintain your professional edge.

7

Cooperative Language

The way service representatives phrase things to hostile customers affects their reactions. Service representatives can sound arrogant, disbelieving, mistrustful, challenging and uncaring. Or, they can sound cooperative, willing to listen and discuss and flexible.

Some words and tones have a confrontational and challenging edge to them, while others are more cooperative and calming. Most individuals are unaware of the speech they use and the impact of their words. They are unaware of the ways they use language and may inadvertently sound combative even when they don't mean to be.

■ IMPLICATIONS — WHAT THIS MEANS TO YOU

Two styles of language can be used in the service environment—confrontational or comforting. It is important for service representatives to be aware of how they voice their thoughts in order to avoid accidentally triggering a hostile reaction from customers or making an already difficult situation worse.

■ STRATEGIES, TIPS & TECHNIQUES TO APPLY

The appropriate use of language impacts the service representative's effectiveness in dealing with his or her customers. Often the choice of words and the tones used are reflective of the service representative's personal attitude towards their client. There are two types of language used by service representatives, each capable of producing markedly different outcomes. These are:

Confrontational Language

Confrontational language is harsh and has the effect of making the customer feel cornered without options. Service representatives using this language display an unwillingness to consider the other person's position and a detrimental rigidity that says they are absolutely right in their beliefs and viewpoints. This language leads customers to believe they have no choices and are to blame for their own problems.

Confrontational language gives customers the perception that there are no alternatives available. It further intensifies their lack of control and desperation in the situation. Additionally, the use of confrontational language tends to encourage the customer to use the same style of language with service representatives. This generally causes the situation to escalate as the use of confrontational language intensifies the level of conflict between the customer and the service representative.

Cooperative Language

When service representatives use cooperative language, customers realize they are not dealing with stereotypical bureaucrats who never admit to being wrong and are uninterested in and uncaring about their problems. Customers understand service representatives are trying to work with them and are on their side, dealing with the problem and making the best of a bad situation.

The use of cooperative language conveys to the customer that service representatives are willing to listen to their position and recognize that they could be wrong. It invites the customer to discuss the problem, rather than challenging them and placing them on the defensive.

Cooperative language has a milder and more collaborative tone. It provides room for choice, tends to blame no one for the problem and allows the customer to save face.

Examples of Confrontational and Cooperative Language

As is evident in the following list, confrontational language tends to be phrased in terms of negative absolutes. It conveys to the customer either that what they are asking is highly unreasonable, or that they are in some way responsible for their own problem.

Confrontational Language
- I can't
- We never
- We always
- You must have
- You must
- You can't
- That's impossible
- You're wrong
- You should have

Cooperative Language
- I don't think I can
- We usually don't
- We try to
- It's possible that
- That hardly ever happens
- I don't think that is going to help you
- Is it possible that
- The best thing to do
- You might try

Service representatives are much better served to phrase their responses to hostile customers in a more equivocal manner that still communicates an essential truth, but in a non-accusatory way that allows the customer "wiggle room."

Including the Customer in the Use of 'We'

Service representatives desire to give the impression that they are working collaboratively with the customer, not against them. As such, they might find it helpful to replace the words "you" and "I" with "we." This gives the psychological impression that service representatives are on the same side of the problem as the customer. It suggests cooperation.

'Hot' Words

Some words and phrases have such emotional meaning for people that no matter how benign the tone of voice, these words will immediately trigger an

insulting and inflammatory reaction. These are terms that service representatives should avoid at all costs, including:
- I don't care.
- Whatever.
- It's not my problem.

There is no way for service representatives to use these phrases and sound cooperative and helpful. It should be noted that when service representatives acknowledge the customer's reaction and responses, and use paraphrasing techniques, repeating hot words and phrases should be avoided.

POINTS TO PONDER — SOMETHING TO THINK ABOUT

1. Are you aware of how confrontational your tone and use of words can be to your customers?
2. Does an understanding of confrontational language provide you with insight into why certain customer situations have deteriorated in the past?

TRAINING ACTIVITY — APPLICATION & ACTION PLAN

List on a sheet of paper all of the typical phrases you use with your customers during the course of a business day. Next to each indicate whether the phrases employ confrontational or cooperative language.

1. Analyze your phrases to determine if your language is genuinely confrontational or cooperative in nature.
2. Change and adapt all confrontational phrases and terms into cooperative language.
3. Practice and incorporate these phrases into your everyday work with customers.
4. Continue this practice for a minimum of 30 days to solidify the habit of utilizing cooperative language.

8

Verbal Self-Defensive Techniques

The primary goal in using self-defense techniques is to regain control of a hostile interaction. These include statements or questions service representatives can use to interrupt a hostile customer's verbal attacks. They are basic self-defense principles that take into account the nature of angry interaction.

Hostile customers tend to dominate the conversation and refuse to respond to normal questions while continuing to talk and interrupt. The use of self-defense techniques is designed to stop the customer so they will begin to respond to the service representative's questions and allow him or her to resolve the situation.

IMPLICATIONS — WHAT THIS MEANS TO YOU

The hostile customer plays by specific rules. As such, the best way to end a personal attack and reassert control is to avoid "playing the game" according to the hostile customer's rules. Service representatives can use specific self-defense techniques to break the rhythm, pace and intensity of a hostile customer's attacks and effectively regain control of the contact.

STRATEGIES, TIPS & TECHNIQUES TO APPLY

Solid self-defense techniques are based on surprise and momentum. When a service representative does what is expected, the hostile customer is prepared and acts almost without thought. If service representatives can freeze the hostile customer in mid-sentence or confuse them, they are able to create an opening to use other effective service techniques. This causes the hostile customer to pause and think.

As relates to momentum, when a hostile customer verbally attacks, it is to the service representative's advantage not to absorb the force of the verbal attack, but—in much the same way a receiving tennis player can use the speed of a 130 mile per hour serve to control the point—use the attack to their advantage by returning.

Within these foundational principles of surprise and momentum, an effective self-defense employs the following strategies:

Use of the 'When' Question

When service representatives use "when" questions, they are responding to an aggressive customer in a way that is not expected. "When" questions can take the form of "When did you start feeling that way?" or, "When did you first notice this occurring?" If the hostile customer answers, service representatives have gained control of the interaction since rather than attempting to dictate the point the person is now reacting to a constructive question that clearly does not discount their feelings or dispute the accuracy of their statement.

Computer Mode

Computer mode is another technique service representatives can use to respond in a way that shows they are listening but does not result in them taking the bait from angry and hostile customers. It is unexpected and tends to disrupt the attack chain by getting the customer to think.

The general form of this response is a neutral statement such as "That's interesting. Some people do think that (whatever the customer has asserted)." The service representative then stops and says nothing further.

Topic Grab

The topic grab involves taking something that the angry customer has said during their tirade and commenting or asking a question about it. This technique distracts angry customers and returns the conversation to a more calm and cooperative state.

The Broken Record Technique

When angry customers refuse to pay attention to what is said, but instead continue with angry and hostile comments, service representatives often find it useful to repeat a pertinent sentence over and over until the angry person finally begins to hear what is being said.

Phone Silence

Telephone conversations have rules. The best way to get angry customers to stop attacking over the phone is to simply say nothing at all. If service representatives can avoid breathing into the phone, or can exclude any noise getting through from their end, this is even more effective. Eventually the angry customer on the other end will stop and say something like, "Are you still there?" and pause for a moment. This provides service representatives the opportunity to say something at the invitation of the angry customer, and has placed them on a more even footing, if not in control.

Agreement

The use of agreement by service representatives is a very powerful self-defense technique. When an angry customer is attacking, they expect service representatives to defend themselves and fight back. When service representatives can find something to agree with, the attacker will be caught off guard. The creation of agreement makes it appear to the customer that the service representative is on their side.

The use of agreement can bring control back to the service representative who seizes upon the opportunity to acknowledge the customer's frustration and offer them help. In many cases, the customer is not calmed down; however, they will begin to scale down their attacks, which then opens the door for service representatives to more effectively do their job.

POINTS TO PONDER — SOMETHING TO THINK ABOUT

1. What self-defense techniques have you found to be effective in dealing with angry and hostile customers?
2. In reviewing these techniques, can you think of situations where one or more would have been effective in handling such a customer?

TRAINING ACTIVITY — APPLICATION & ACTION PLAN

List the typical hostile customer attacks you have experienced on a sheet of paper.

1. Create specific responses to each of these personal attacks using the self-defensive techniques of surprise and momentum taught within this lesson, including:
   - Use of the 'When' Question
   - Computer Mode
   - Topic Grab
   - The Broken Record Technique
   - Silence
   - Agreement
2. Refine your responses and create a list that can be easily referred to when dealing with angry and hostile customers.
3. Practice these techniques and role-play with associates until you are confident with your responses and polished in their application.
4. Use and apply these responses as often as possible until they become natural.

About the Author

Timothy F. Bednarz, Ph.D. is CEO of the American Management Development Group, Inc. For over 20 years he has researched, designed and authored hundreds of learning and development programs used by Fortune 1000 companies.

He is also the author of *Great! What Makes Leaders Great. What They Did, How They Did It and What You Can Learn from It* (2011).

Speaking Availability

Timothy F. Bednarz, Ph.D. is available for speaking engagements for your next meeting or association event. He can be contacted at 800-654-4935 or by e-mail at timothy.bednarz@majorium.com.

Bulk Sales

Bulk sales of this book or any other titles available from Majorium Business Press. Inquiries can be directed to sales@majorium.com, or by phone at 800-6654-4935.

Quick Order Form

Fax orders: 715-342-1118. Send this form.

Telephone orders: Call 800-654-4935 toll-free. Have your credit card ready.

Email orders: sales@majorium.com

Postal orders: Majorium Business Press, 2025 Main Street, Stevens Point, WI 54481, USA.

Please send the following books:

_____

_____

_____

_____

Please send more FREE information on:

❏ Catalog   ❏ Speaking/Seminars   ❏ Mailing Lists   ❏ Consulting

Name: _____

Address: _____

City: _____ State: _____ Zip: _____

Telephone: _____

Email address: _____

Sales tax: Please add 5.5% for products shipped to Wisconsin addresses.

Shipping by air:

United States: $4.00 for first book and $2.00 for each additional product.

International: $9.00 for first book; $5.00 for each additional product (estimate).

Made in the USA
San Bernardino, CA
14 May 2014